Vanishing Acts

Vanishing Acts

Poems by Michael McFee

GNOMON PRESS

LCCC NUMBER 89-80713

ISBN 0-917788-38-9

Published by Gnomon Press,
P.O. Box 475, Frankfort,
Kentucky 40602-0475

Cover drawing by Leah Palmer Preiss

To the memory of my mother,
LUCY FARMER MCFEE

CONTENTS

I. *KINDERSZENEN*

II. *IMAGINARY ELEGIES*

III. *THE ELM*

ACKNOWLEDGMENTS

Thanks to these magazines, their editors and readers, for first
   publishing these poems:

The New Yorker: "Snow Goat"
Poetry: "First Radio," "Bach, Beethoven, Brahms, Mendelssohn,
   Mozart, Schubert, and Schumann," "Shooting Baskets at Dusk,"
   "Ever After," "Cold Quilt"
Hudson Review: "The Picture," "Floor Furnace," "Reading in the
   Tulip Tree," "Stamp Album"
Virginia Quarterly Review: "Family Reunion Near Grape Creek
   Church, Four Miles West of Murphy, N.C., 1880," "Sliding
   Rock"
Crescent Review: "The Elm"
Greensboro Review: "The Minors"
St. Andrews Review: "Backwards Through the Baptist Hymnal"
Sewanee Review: "Thomas Wolfe in a Treehouse"
Iris: "Recurrent Dream"
Carolina Quarterly: "Uncle Homer Meets Carl Sandburg"
Southern Poetry Review: "Kick the Can"
Three Rivers Poetry Journal: "World Without Men"
Southern Humanities Review: "Long Story Short"

"Cold Quilt" was printed as a broadside by Mill Springs Press (New
Market, TN); "Bach, Beethoven, Brahms, Mendelssohn, Mozart,
Schubert, and Schumann" was printed as a broadside by Iron
Mountain Press (Emory, VA). Thanks to Danny Marion and Bob
Denham, respectively.

Thanks also to the National Endowment for the Arts, the Ingram
Merrill Foundation, and the North Carolina Arts Council for
fellowships in poetry; and to Robert Morgan, Scott Byrd, and the
Critz-folk for critical encouragement.

· I ·

KINDERSZENEN

THE PICTURE

I am strapped into stiff lederhosen
sent by an army uncle's mother-in-law,
tied into freshly whited dress shoes,
posed before the canoe-sized window box
lousy with dime store petunias,
crying:

my earliest memory. And here I am
again, tugging at the foreign leather,
the buckles, the buttons and ornaments
"carved from a wild stag's horn,"
begging the Kodak to look away
please

as I do from the same frayed plot
year after year, in new Easter suits
and caps, in first-day-of-school shoes,
clutching baskets, Bibles, lunchboxes
beside my sister, our eyes saying
help

no matter how hard we smile. Waiting
for the shutter's faint snip to release us,
I taste mothballs and juniper bushes,
I feel my body grow odd in its clothes,
I seem to hear somebody laughing at
me.

RECURRENT DREAM

I am perched on the felt backseat
of mom's station wagon, my twin in age.
"We will go to the park for a picnic,"
she says, starting across the bridge

so rotten I can see water through it,
the river so distended by downpours
that its banks are a muddy memory,
that Boy Scout Island has disappeared.

"Watch out!" she shouts halfway across,
but the pothole has already shocked
me off the seat through a rusty cavity
in the floorboard, through the pocked

rickety bridge, through the dark air
into the river sweeping me like debris
downstream, choking me with its loud
brown grip, good as drowned already.

And then I look up from my dying
to see mother firmly paddle forward
in a bright yellow life raft, slicker and hat,
offering me the fat blade of her oar.

FLOOR FURNACE

We'd shiver and chatter in our sheets
until it stirred, an arthritic pet
haunting the dirt basement.

We'd listen to the snap, crackle, pop
of every antique joint, waiting
as it talked itself awake,

then sprint to the faint living room
when it finally began breathing
another day into being.

We'd loiter on the grave-sized grate
in the Motorola's silver glow,
saturated by radiance

so long our sleepy soles were scored
like waffles, my sister's gown
a tender flannel tent.

All summer long it would hibernate
under the crooked braided rug,
but at killing frost

we'd uncover the floor furnace again
and pray for a holiday snowfall
deep as that heat's rising.

FIRST RADIO

A plastic transistor from Japan,
aqua, with black vinyl straps, some chrome trim,
an ear-sized speaker, dials like nails—
perfect in the pocket as a pack of cigarettes,
its hidden heart pulsing over mine.

At lunch, at recess, on the bus,
each fall I'd strain to crack the glamorous code
of the World Series, pinching bright flags
of foil around the bent antenna,
hoping to attract Mantle or Koufax or Gibson.

And at night, planting it under my pillow
like a tooth, like a magic seed,
I'd fall asleep to top-40 big-city dee-jays
bouncing off cloud cover thousands of miles away,
better than any answered prayer.

BACH, BEETHOVEN, BRAHMS, MENDELSSOHN, MOZART, SCHUBERT, AND SCHUMANN

Seven years in the cramped hot heaven
of the choir loft, for seven statuettes,
an ensemble of immortal shrunken heads
whose music we were never allowed to sing
unless simplified into Baptist hymns.

How I hated the angelic robe, its girlish
skirts and sleeves and bow! How bored I was
staring at the endless backside of sermons,
Mrs. Reynolds omniscient in the sanctuary,
ready to report our least whisper or giggle.

And so I'd daydream, flooding the church
until we could cannonball from the balcony,
exchanging the pews for a parquet court,
converting the pulpit into a concert stage
for the only local appearance by the Beatles.

But I loved those busts, the strange wedge
of their torsos, their fancy jackets and ties,
their long hair and even sideburns or beards,
the fingered relief of their foreign names,
the music in their vacant gazes, dreaming . . .

READING IN THE TULIP TREE

Scaling my library of air,
through leaves idly riffled by wind
   and scrutinized by the sun,
I'd climb till the tree's pliant crown
   could bear no more, wedge
my crotch into some soft gray crook,
   take a book from my teeth,
and read another afternoon away.

My mother, the nervous curator,
   would chime from the screen
every quarter hour: "Honey? Honey?
   Are you all right up there?"
The tree nodded yes, all its leaves
   whispered yes, our old dog
asleep in my shadow flickering below
   managed a friendly whimper,

but I closed my eyes to the words
   and let the poplar sway me,
a minor character in Chapter 64
   of some unfinishable novel
but, for a moment, the hazy focus
   of all this bouyant light
from below and above and around me,
   the sweet fire of tulip bloom.

SHOOTING BASKETS AT DUSK

He will never be happier than this,
lost in the perfectly thoughtless motion
of shot, rebound, dribble, shot,

his mind removed as the gossipy swallows
that pick and roll, that give and go
down the school chimney like smoke in reverse

as he shoots, rebounds, dribbles, shoots,
the brick wall giving the dribble back
to his body beginning another run

from foul line, corner, left of the key,
the jealous rim guarding its fickle net
as he shoots, rebounds, dribbles, shoots,

absorbed in the rhythm that seems to flow
from his fingertips to the winded sky
and back again to this lonely orbit

of shot, rebound, dribble, shot,
until he is just a shadow and a sound
though the ball still burns in his vanished hands.

KICK THE CAN

If you're It, you kneel with your hand over the can
like a lid sealing the fate of your dozen friends,
counting to 100 in an auctioneer's slick slur.
You snap your eyes open to a realtor's photograph,
yards and carports purified of children, everything empty
except the air quivering with dusky whispers.
You start to circle outwards like a nervous setter,
tethered to the dull still life of the black-eyed peas,
emptied several hours ago for your hurried supper.

If you're not, you scatter like filings from a magnet
into backyards, preferably the Dixons' with its paradise
of half-full beer cans, wrecked Plymouths, moldy Playboys.
Or you slump under an oil barrel with Marsha Shope,
the one girl with breasts yet, already bored with boys
her age, muffing buttons and snaps like easy ground balls.
Or you stand lookout for It, your dim friends lolling,
skinny dipping in the heated pool of wide summer nights,
careless of consequences until steps at the corner gutter

flush you like a quail from hiding, hunter and hunted
twinned in a grim race across the dew-slick grass
toward the base siphoning the living daylight
into itself, a pair of arrows closing on the bull's eye,
a couple of shadows jockeying for position,
the captured ones cheering your dying legs on
till you stretch and your bare toe dents ribbed tin
and you hear the hollow music of a perfect end-over-end
and you know, as you pitch into darkness, that you are free.

STAMP ALBUM

The world lay filleted on its cover,
stamps flying like flags from the capitals.

I opened the album to Monaco,
laid a rich commemorative over its ghost.

The page seemed to quiver with color,
with the exotic mint perfume of the princess.

Not even machines would dare cancel
such exquisite taste, such high denomination.

The world seemed to come when ordered
to my imperial desk, itemized for mounting

in the museum I bent to every night,
lost in the crackle of glassine envelopes,

the perforation perfect as gear-teeth,
the mystery of those watermarks made visible

by the lamp as I hinged stamps, row after row—
those bright windows into distant lives.

EVER AFTER

It swings on its gold ball chain like a rabbit's foot,
   a truncated pyramid of molded green plastic
the size of a pack of Life Savers: a Delmar Colorscope.

I hold it to my glasses, squint toward the reading lamp,
   complete the textbook cone of sight—and there
I am, mummified since first grade in this tomb's base,

my shirt's starchy collar cinched tight, my hair still
   freshly parted and anointed with Vitalis,
my eyes the same hopeful tone of blue as the background.

I gently pinch this telescope onto the past, an appraiser
   contemplating the value of what he's seen.
I peek again, a child at the porthole of a theater door.

Is this how we fix our scenes from childhood, locked
   into vacuums of sharp but inaccurate color,
a dozen novelty items for some village nostalgia shop?

Could this be how my mother, so unexpectedly among the
   cushioned dead, sees me now, pressing my life
to her diminished eyes, squinting back toward the light?

· II ·

IMAGINARY ELEGIES

COLD QUILT

Our clear-eyed guide said it is the slick
cotton that makes quilts cold. I wonder
if it isn't the enduring dowry of bitterness
stitched into them that makes us shiver,
as in that quilt (unfit for hanging) handed
down to me from my father's mother, begun
the day her husband died, a lifelong lament

composed of old suits and shirts he'd worn,
threaded to her leftover dresses, its design—
each pane a basket of memorial flowers,
a dozen loud triangles tipped on their sides—
a stiff pastiche of grief and the solitary
nights spent trying to transform their bad luck
into something useful, used. No busy bee

touched that quilt. Her life became a patchwork
of quilted plenty, her backyard a dormitory
of vegetable beds, her table a dazzling pattern
of cakes and pies. But she stayed skinny
and wrapped herself in the plain handmade cocoon
of that death-quilt every night, even when
she began to fade in her children's spare beds.

At the funeral home, my uncle the soldier
draped her coffin with it, prayed, then handed
that life's flag to me, compactly folded, her
crooked stitches and nearly-rotten panes still
tenacious after half a century, the sheep
I count now in the inherited dark, her cold quilt
a poultice I spread on my chest before sleep.

WORLD WITHOUT MEN

When my fat aunt's husband finally died
she turned to bowling. Her upper room
gleamed like a royal tomb with trophies,
they gilded both halls, the parlor mantel,
the bathroom, you could navigate the house
on a cloudy night by their low gold light

as I still do in dreams of that place,
so empty of men, all dead or disappeared,
so full of smell: my long-widowed grandmother
in the kitchen, coaxing the stove with feet
to mint another cake, Aunt Messalina upstairs
dazzling the bathroom with gift bubbles
and her toothless rendition of the blues,
the other widows and spinsters and girls
filling her spare trophies with cut flowers.

In one dream I am eavesdropping at the door
when my bathing aunt calls, "Come in, honey!"
I fear the judgment of some prudish god

but go in anyway, blinded for an instant
by steam and cigarette smoke and bubbles.
The first thing I can make out is a trophy
on the tiles, brimming with hours of ash;
the second is Messalina's wavy silver hair,
poised in that radiance like a ritual headdress

never taken off. "Let me show you something,"
she says, and props her legs, huge as tusks,
on the faucets. "Once, when I was just about
your big sister's age, I hitched a ride out
to Christcrest, where my fellow was working
as a counselor for the summer. Well, we did
what young folks will be doing, and afterwards
there in the woods, in that little chapel
of soft pine needles and late afternoon sun,

we promised to marry each other, and sealed
our oath by taking some leaves of poison oak
and writing on these thighs, in big letters,

first my name"—she traced it again—"then
his, so they'd be right on top of each other
under my dress, whenever I crossed my legs!
Before that weekend, I'd never been allergic
to poison oak or ivy or sumac: we expected
a mild reaction at best, a slight outline

of letters, a ghostly pledge no one else
would ever know was there. Well, something
set me off instead, and I'd barely got home
before my thighs began to blister and itch
like crazy. I filled this tub with cold water
and baking soda and soaked for several hours
but it only got worse, until I had to call
mama, and she called the doctor, and nobody
said much but everybody had a pretty good idea

what had happened. I had to rub these thighs
with an ointment that smelled like dead skunks
for weeks, and had to walk bowlegged so long

your daddy called me 'cowgirl.' Can you feel
the scars there?" I could, and still can.
I asked her if they got married. "Lord, no!
But you know, honey, I don't regret a thing."
And she flung back her great sterling head
and laughed at the memory, at the dentures

sunk in a glass by the sink, at the spectacles
steaming beside them, at the athlete's feet
and branded legs she buried under the water.
In that dream, the whole houseful of women
with no man to pity or tend except me
laughed at my aunt's laughing, drifting
like a sweet aroma downstairs, saturating
every molecule in the place with pleasure,
that house my shelter from the fallout

of fear learned at school and at home,
a world without men where no weekly drills
were needed. But grandmother eventually died

and her spinster sisters moved to Florida,
and Messalina suffered a tremendous stroke
that trimmed 200 pounds, leaving her hair
like flat pewter, a cap melted to her scalp.
Out-of-town strangers bought the house
and chopped down the cherry tree and arbor,

planting a yard where the garden had been.
In another dream, I am alone in the pantry
dug out beneath the back porch, a preserve
of preserves. Someone has shut the trap door
and is sitting on it, but I am not worried
there in the jar-bright earth, surrounded
by the sweet spoils of a summer, the smell
of dirt and apples and potatoes, the cool
glow of food, a pair of bowling trophies

full of herbs. Then I hear a familiar voice:
Are you down there, honey? Can I come in?
And then I stand in that grave and wake.

LONG STORY SHORT

You write for facts about family history
and she says, "Better people I never knew,
they were the true salt of the earth, honey."

You press for real detail: "What about Drew?"
"He *was* odd—mama called him 'my foundling'—
but loyal. He'd lay down his life for you."

You visit, but her stories make poor kindling
for any ancestral fire, her memories mild
as an old stone from too-frequent handling.

You rise. "Wait." She worries the bureau, piled
with tracts and prescriptions, flushing a flock
of pictures. "I got no use for these, child."

So you reach for the evidence, its dim shocks
like twittering myths from an inlaid box.

FAMILY REUNION NEAR GRAPE CREEK CHURCH, FOUR MILES WEST OF MURPHY, N.C., 1880

Everybody moved. Only that background shed
is focused, its roof a black hat for the ladies
clustered toward the rear of this sober choir
behind the bearded blurs in Confederate dress,
the infants and the witch-like matriarch.

And nobody smiled, unwilling to suffer
minutes of breathless muscle before a camera
omniscient as the Lord or a ready predator,
forgetting that the involuntary subtle pulse
of simply being human and alive would erase

this effort at a record, sure as the weather
would wash its hands on their soapstone graves
until no text was left, sure as bitter years
would blight their genealogy with stillbirths,
death in the service, "bean lodged in throat."

Even the trees above moved. This might as well
be any family, Adam's fallen clan, regathered
outside Paradise for their farewell picnic.
What curse or promise do they bear, these men
with radiant chests and women brightly buttoned,

that tall unbiblical couple near the border,
her birdlike hands poised in some peculiar sign,
his right hand not sheathed over the starchy heart
but pressed to his temple, sharp index finger
cocked in some elaborate parody of suicide?

Vague old ghosts, "four miles west of Murphy"
might as well be four miles east of Manteo:
the dumbfounded verge of nowhere, a landscape
lost to heaven's shutter since the deluge
or buried for decades now under dammed water.

AN EXPEDITION, DURING THE GREAT WAR, BY THOMAS EDISON, HENRY FORD, AND HARVEY FIRESTONE

Apollo, Mercy, and Vulcan
descended to Asheville for the climate
and its new Inn, built with the profits
    from Doctor Grove's patent medicine.
    He owned the whole of Sunset Mountain,
rough-quarried its granite to rusticize
his resort, sent the subtly publicized
    trinity there on expedition.

Apollo, Mercury, and Vulcan
traveled light—a marquee party tent,
six-course evening meals, six manservants
    to pitch and strike, to tend and run,
    retrieving game their masters stunned
though they never skinned or ate the prize,
saving each one for stuffing, those eyes
    glassy with preoccupation.

Apollo, Mercury, and Vulcan
talked of the War, its lucky impact
on morale, markets, union contracts.
    And as they spoke, their guide, a man
    who might have called me great-grandson,
shook his head by the outer fire, despising
those millionaire bastards, their enterprising,
    their labs and plants and plantations.

Apollo, Mercury, and Vulcan
vacation elsewhere now. And summers I rise
from a rich friend's pool on Sunset, my eyes
    stinging for that imaginary person.

THOMAS WOLFE IN A TREEHOUSE

Hard to hide when you're a giant, a prodigal
come home, beset by curious tourists and family
    and words, the words that never stop swarming
    no matter how deep you write, the cabin floor
swamped by manuscript. So you sneak to sanctuary

    here, seizing the pine like an amorous grizzly
and shinnying to hidden eminence. How you love
    the Swannanoa flowing so sweetly below,
    the dance pavilion cradled in its elbow,
the couple who cannot imagine you swaying above,

    humming their tune, waiting for the New York train
to puff across the valley, piercing this pastoral
    with its wail, the dusky chord of a world
    beyond. As you smoke, the royal mountains fold
their tents for the night, the Asheville Special

    grieves at the station, and you suddenly imagine
this all gone, the boat-gay lake silted, the steam
    engine still as the nimble couple in the riverside
    cemetery, your own extinct bones beyond hiding,
pine bark and cigarette butts and treehouse frame

    and writing cabin all forgotten. You sit, whittle
some letters in the boy-smooth floor, remember
    your first train trip to Chapel Hill almost
    twenty years ago, that girl with the pentecost
of hair, how you plunged your hand in its thick fire

without thinking; how—in the ink-black middle
of Piedmont nowhere—she had you bounced, her white
    dress refining the window like that pile of novel
    in the cabin below; how the mourning doves will
soothe a lovesick footsore freshman all night

    under a roadside pine. Soon you will abandon
your watchtower in memory's rickety caboose,
    stretching and laughing a train-loud blast
    that will haunt the pregnant air at the dance
where you hike again in the owl-lit dark and lose

    the curse of speech, cured of its consumption.
And years later, trespassing, suspended above
    that same scene, my father's brother will find
    the message your pocket knife left behind,
two million words reduced to two: LOST   LOVE.

UNCLE HOMER MEETS CARL SANDBURG

After the nervous young professor read "Grass"
aloud to his G.I.-packed class, then said
that the author now lived only a few counties away,
my mother's renegade brother resolved to speak his thanks
to this poet who piled his lines high with bodies
and understood the need simply to get on with our work.

For almost four years, Uncle Homer's sole work
had been to urge his bad feet across Europe, its grass,
its mud, its rotten roads. *I've seen enough bodies
to last me nine lifetimes* was all he ever said
about it. His dreams flickered with the skeletal thanks
of prisoners whose camps they freed, so far away
from the tranquil Blue Ridge.
                  And so he found a way
to borrow a friend's new Olds and beg off work
that weekend. The drive was a soldier's belated thanks-
giving, the road orbiting Pisgah, the goat-grass
glowing in the pasture below Sandburg's house. Homer said
I cover all as he parked between the sleeping bodies
of roadside hounds.
              He tried to imagine the bodies
that could cover this field, the stench drifting away
into the safe hazy mountains. His teacher had said
this mansion was first a rich lowlander's, later to work
as Confederate Treasurer, until money was like grass:
"Sandburg made his fortune on the Lincoln books—thanks
be to irony!—then bought the place."

Many thanks,
Mr. Sandburg, practiced Homer, scattering the prize bodies
of the Chikaming herd, his eyes lost in soft grass.
Suddenly, like a grenade, he heard, "Hey! Get away!"
He turned to see Carl Sandburg with a stick. "Your work,
sir—" he began, but the flushed poet charged him. "I said
GET AWAY, you!"
              Homer slipped backwards in shit, said
shit and scrambled away, shouting over his shoulder, "Thanks
for 'Grass,' sir! Great poem!" It was difficult work
escaping that goat-faced old shepherd, their bodies
a bad vaudeville gag, but my black-sheep uncle pulled away
at last from that shocking head vanishing into the grass.

Homer said he admired Sandburg for that chase, their bodies'
rhyme a kind of thanks, a grace that wouldn't fade away
like dated work or words raised over weed-choked grass.

SLIDING ROCK

I never saw my blind uncle
    without a cigar, it was his ashy cane,
a cheap way of keeping the world
    blinded, breathless, at shouting distance.

One night on our porch he inhaled
    fiercely, his square face an open furnace,
        and billowed, "Know what I'd like
            to see again before I die? Sliding Rock."

And so we went, one Labor Day,
    across the county steeping in rich fumes
from Enka's plant, the nylon made
    to smooth the legs of ladies in fine homes,

climbing above our stale valley
    into the old Vanderbilt forest. "It's coming!"
        My uncle stuck out his head to smell
        like a pickup hound. "Everything's getting cool."

We parked where the Davidson thinned
    and spilled down a slick slope of bedrock
bigger than a barn roof, ending
    in a deep pool at the foot, hemlock-dark,

cold enough to give you the bends
    at the bottom of each slide, a body-shocking
        baptism by immersion. "This is it,"
        my uncle said to the sound. "Let's get undressed."

I helped him into trunks, a pair
   my father molted when he was still single.
My uncle kept his shades and cigar,
   a fresh one trimmed and lit with much ritual

there in the slimy bathhouse. I was sure
   people would laugh at him, unnaturally pale
      as a cavern-fish, when we descended
      the stones to the holy river. But no one did.

Teenagers restless as otters
   were fluming down the heart of Sliding Rock,
ignoring the insidious potholes
   that mined the limits of their breakneck track.

Summer lingered, but the water
   felt like a midwinter draft, glacial, tragic.
      My uncle seized me, shouting, "Hey!"
      I turned back toward the bank, but he said, "Wait.

Let's go." My father waved from the pool
   below. I sat my rigid uncle in the current
and whispered, "I'm right behind you,"
   and shoved him like a dogsled, and we went

down that hill quick as Eskimos
   past the rooted audience
      of our family
      and trees

through water colder than any word,
   my uncle dropping his cigar onto his legs,
me clinging to his back like a curse,
   both of us exploding into my father's chest

and underwater, once, twice, a third
   time, forgetting how to breathe, my uncle's head
      snapping backwards like a hooked bass
      with his blank eyesockets and his wide dead eyes.

SNOW GOAT

Stirred by the snow's rare erasure, my sister
hikes across backyards quiet as a bedroom
into the ruin-rich woods where Jack kissed her,
then disappeared beyond the briers and gloom.

Who cares? she says, skiing shallow ravines
behind the vacant sausage plant. *What a bore.*
I hope he gets killed in Korea with the Marines
or Army. Nothing could surprise me anymore.

Then the snow at her elbow says *bah* and there
he is, shocking as God, white, his slitted eye
golden with curiosity. He tongues the bare
salt lick of her hand, and she starts to cry,
fearing his cloven hooves and her desire
sharp as those horns whetted on the wire.

APRIL 4, 1968

My cousin prayed King would die
and he did. She was 13, unlucky,

a lonely girl who square-danced
instead of dating. At practice

that rainy night she whispered
in her partner's lifted ear,

"I'm glad he's dead, ain't you?"
That country boy's face grew

peculiar, warping like a trick
mirror, its surface flickering

between uneasy pleasure and fear.
Less than five years before

she'd traced a maudlin likeness
of JFK on onionskin, kissed

his blue lips, wept, then pressed
it in the family Bible under Deaths

even though she'd already boasted
on the bus that her folks voted

for Nixon. Later she would canvass
support for McGovern, embarrassed

by her ignorant parents' politics,
angry that she somehow missed

all the wars, good causes, rights,
the clear allegiances. But that night

she danced each step with vicious joy,
her body required by all the boys

who spun and lifted it and clutched
her to their chests, their sweaty touch

sheltering her from that dark man
who deserved to die, his last sermon

crackling across the TV's altar
a threat, she felt somehow, to her

undeveloped future, a shadow
cast on her crisp crinoline's glow

despite the footlights, the shuffle
of her feet not quite muffling

that echo drifting from the empty
back row of the chained balcony.

THE MINORS

The night's a humidor from the fumes
   of curing, tobacco
the tie that binds chain-smoking hecklers

who forklift hogsheads on the day shift,
   then drift wifeless
into the park, beer-sour, chronically dim,

to ruminant players, spitting and plotting
   the astronomical streaks
that will lift them from the quicksand

of this hick league. One boldface entry in
   the slim column
of memory's indelible statistics—that's all

they want: our impetuous bonus-baby-faced
   pitcher gone wild,
his lame manager en route to the mound

cursing that reckless career-ending slide,
   their bitter batter
a Series star before injuries and drugs,

the thirty-year-old Dominican shortstop
   whose American girl,
no longer loitering by the players' entrance

offering anyone anything for a quick ticket
        out of town,
rehearses for close-ups in the wives' box,

a young ump whose dress shirt has sprouted
        wings of sweat,
sportswriters sounding the Underwood's bell,

kids waiting for home runs on the kudzu bank
        behind the drunken
ad-loud fence . . . . Our best schemes for escape

often fail, leaving us bus-tired and broke,
        thin doomed pennants
of smoke sighed toward a balding ballfield,

the past another flattened Labor Day mound
        in Medicine Hat,
Thetford Mines, Kinston, a hundred Mudvilles:

no clippings but no shame in that. To designated
        hitters and critics
the majority of our leagues or lives or lines

may seem minor, but from the reserved seats
        of their condescension
they miss the subtle moral of these bodies,

the grace of a game which can redeem even
    the most desperate
instant in late-inning bleachers or bullpen,

one report of bat miraculously tangent to ball
    sufficient to lift
scattered fanatics to dead-sleepy feet, the minor

key of individual lives forgotten in a chord of
    raw local color
as the ball rises toward old wilted glory

and tireless nightjars shag flies already
    thick as memories
against the high lights of the mind's diamond.

BACKWARDS THROUGH THE BAPTIST HYMNAL

for Annie Dillard and Belinda

What glorious fossils from the faulty brain,
impressed by rote in remote sanctuaries
or around more distant campfires: what relics,
hauled protestant into our killing air
to demonstrate the double miracle—*memory*
and *song*: what swarm of cicadas, dormant
for 17 years, rising to plague the equinox
with "Is Your All on the Altar?", "Throw Out
the Lifeline!", "Low in the Grave He Lay,"
"At Calvary," "Blessed Assurance," "He Lives!"

From the least scrap, whole hymns accumulate,
words, melodic skeletons, ghostly descants.
B. plies the organ with its comic stops,
Annie gravely brays the melody, while I go
fishing for that plain bass line, surfacing
during refrains to croak, "send the light,"
"I surrender all," "it is well," "by and by."
We backslide through the low-church standards,
proclaiming an unreformed text: plenty of sin
and saving blood, no hootenanny gospel yet.

This may seem a joke to late-chore neighbors,
to God, even to us when I accidentally mash
the swing key when the roll is called up yonder.
It may be an offense against honest silence.
But what could possibly be better than writing
something to be read and sung until finally
anonymous, licked smooth by the flock, something
turned to so often the page is finger-stained,
something, however flawed, that may one night
suddenly come to other tongues as praise?

· III ·

THE ELM

THE ELM

We came home from England to find the elm
fallen, its great trunk (once solid shade)
segmented like a cathedral pylon, xylem
and phloem of cold stone clustering upward
into gravity-baffling columns, arches, pediments,
domes, now felled into the shadow of itself,
heavy drums scattered as if never assembled
or, worse, toppled in some puritan rage to level,
some radical conceit. The pines, skinny courtiers
swayed by the least breeze, lean backwards
in astonishment at new sun on their trunks,
the sudden gap in apostolic succession of elm,
divine right of seed. Any extinction ends
in a single death, any death bears the possible
germ of extinction, the dissolution of an order
ancient and charitable as *Ulmus americana*.

It died at the top, like Swift. When July leaves
wilted unseasonably, and the elm began molting
gradually larger branches nearer the house,
one night shocking us with a burglar-loud limb
on our bedroom roof, we knew something was wrong
and asked Mr. Green our neighbor, gifted with plants.
"Looks like Dutch elm disease. You know, when I's
a boy and we'd walk into town Saturdays, they was
rows and rows of the tallest elm-trees you ever saw
alongside the road, just like walking in Duke Chapel,
you know. And then the blight come in the mid-50's,
about the time you's born, and soon won't *nothing*
but a line of stumps, about high as a man's thigh,
far as you could see. Looked like a whole different place.
They planted maples, but it won't the same. —Nothing
else *to* do, though, once the blight gets started, but
take out the whole tree. Good thing you only got one."

Still, remembering the lepers healed, the once-blind
who saw men as trees walking, we stalled like children
with a failing parent, praying for miracles, remission
and revival. (Can trees feel pain? Can the cardinal
sin, the moaning dove know grief?) When we left, the elm
was spared but still upright, tree-true. So was Mr. Green.

Today I performed a post-mortem on the elm
or what's left of it, after the chainsaw gang
stripped the upper tree, leaving plugs of trunk
heavy as concrete culverts, and one tremendous
branching aorta-joint. Dimensions at hip-height:
circumference 101″, diameter 30″. (Could archaeologists,
given that bare data, reconstruct the vanished elm
dinosaur-like, from a scrap or two raise the balance
unimaginably large, a full-scale papier-mâché model
to fill a wing at the natural history museum?)
Recounting rings from their epicenter, I figure
53—the age of our now-exposed house—and discover
the heartwood solid to sight and heel: a sprinkling
of discoloration, but no tragic flaw, no hollows
or rotten core, no apparent cancer. Idly, I pry off
some bark—then drop it, aghast at the etchings
on the inner surface, the science-fiction circuitry
uncovered there: the beetle's fatal brood galleries,
larval tunnels radiating like sinister tentacles
of some prehistoric millipedes from the Cambrian
or fossil hieroglyphics inscribed under cambium,
a scroll of lost cabala beneath a cork veneer.
How intricate the awful pattern, curious as chalky
land-art excavated for the gods' pleasure, mystery
to the future! To read this braille by fingertip
is to feel the sober tremens of countless bugs
boiling under chilled skin, flaying from within,
your frame whittled into scrimshaw, instrument
for a funeral tattoo.

43

The elm lies in broken state
on a bed of sawdust, one whiplash pine turning
copper with fear at the sight. As with any death,
what is most remarkable is most absent: the form
of the departed, its gap left in the natural order,
the vast elm-shaped vacancy remaining. Where once
it scrimmaged with sweetgum and minor growth
for sunlight, rain, elbow room, eminence over all—
a canyon of air yawns, a well of space formerly
brimming with elm. You can trace the tree's shape
in the growth allotted its neighbors, squinting
almost sketch it back into place, see its fluent
vase-like tracery against the sky. Now, nothing
intercepts messages from sun, star or streetlight,
late train and siren, car door, storm coming, going:
nothing to translate the world into that language
we can't understand but simply can't live without.

1930: Dutch Elm disease, contagion of shade-world,
first reported in America, when our tree was still
a seedling and our house barely framed, a sanctuary
of sympathetic timber, sacred to young local druids.
Elm timber was favored then for automobile bodies
as it had been for shipbuilding in the New World:
it didn't splinter, bent well, and stayed strong.
Until the epidemic. Within a generation, native elms
were doomed. What a future senator might imagine as
Communist subversion, a Red infection of our trees,
or what some prophet might have called a plague
visited on God's nation for its shameful sin,
was in plain fact a fungus spread by bark beetles
in a kind of lethal pollination, tree by tree.
Hardened arteries followed, the flow of phloem
and xylem choked by expanding fungus, each tree
dying at its surface of sapwood, limb by limb,
until branches collapsed or had to be amputated,
gangrenous. Desperate communities tried anything,
including miraculous DDT, which did stop beetles
but also birds and the other warm-blooded links
in food chains. Some tried seduction, one pheromone
"almost as attractive as virgin females." Nothing
worked: if beetles couldn't fly to nearby hosts,
they hitchhiked on railroads, highways, ships,
just like they came, as stowaways on lumber
from Holland, where the disease had leveled
all their dike trees. Or a picturesque elm-row
shared the fungus through fused roots: no shelter
deep enough to escape this fallout, this cancer
spreading its deadly rumor, lightening limbs and trunk.

Mr. Green died of cancer, too, his succumbing
equally sudden and numbing. He was born far out
in flat country, one of many kids quick and dead
for whom a good tree was treasure, entertainment,
shelter from sun for cattle and family, fire
for winter stove or hearth. He worked his life
in small Southern cities, not marrying until late,
then built a trim brick house in this suburb, far
from the farm's original frame. As a gardener,
Mr. Green was famous to his neighbors: weeds were
as far from his garden's mind as sin from a saint's.
"How's your garden coming!" he would cry, blaming
the weather for our own failure. We rose to praise
the cornucopia of his bean arbor, towering tomatoes,
greens and potatoes and squashes, and he proudly
gave us the guided tour again, straining our arms
with produce. It was his talent and his pleasure,
our pleasure, too. I find myself scouting for clues
of his stirring, the chimes on his toolshed door,
or that fainter signal of gentleman's cologne
on the breeze. I half-expect to look to my left
past the window tree no longer there, to his garden,
and see him hoeing and humming in the fine clothes
he always wore to work, white shirt buttoned full,
high gray pants and hat, hearing aid turned down—
rapt in his rhythm, calmly plotting the resurrection.

Mr. Green was tall, handsome, steadfast as a tree.
Bluebird nests were his sole topic of gossip,
though he gave alms to beggar-birds at feeders.
Just before we left he helped me notch a pine
and raise a fresh rail. Afterwards, I pointed out
a gang of high-pitched migrating cedar waxwings
sharing berries down the length of a stark elm-limb.
"What about that!" he whispered, folding his gloves.

He always tried to give away more than he grew.
Now his cold frame is broken, bolting, gone to weed.

According to our landlord, it took the elm crew
90 minutes to get it down, 90 seconds to cancel
each year's slow growth. We might like to imagine
its fall heroic, a fabled Greek yielding the field
after numerous wounds, or a defiant giant stunned
by sleight of hand, collapsing with seismic force,
his inconceivable death sending terror-tremors
through the assembled enemy,

        though in sad fact
it's probably more like a pack of snarling dogs
wearing down a sick old champion inch by inch. . . .
After the chainsaw din, a lull, then a heart-
wrenching splinter as the newly-streamlined tree
(still riddled with beetles) topples awkwardly
through the undergrowth, splitting gums, spraining
stray limbs, skinning flaky bystanders alive—
the transition from column to classical ruin,
from upright tree to matching stump-and-log set,
taking less time than a guilty afternoon nap.

I woke up disoriented last night, too far west
after travel, zones out of phase. So much light
thawed the dark, I thought we were in Scotland
at the equinox, sun and moon the horizon's foci.
Then I remembered: the elm was no longer there
to baffle the brilliant pole-lamp, to provide
a rehearsal perch for the insomniac mockingbird.
And then I remembered my dream. I was slugging
the still-standing elm with a massive sledgehammer,
trying to crack the trunk. It resisted like granite
but I kept swinging, and soon the bark fractured
perfect as glass, the tree wholly hollow. Inside,
small animals were hibernating, chipmunks, birds,
a family of rabbits, squirrels. I lifted them out
one by one, then stepped through the lanciform door
into the chamber where we hid our childhood away,
time suspended in that echoing wood. The stone elm
healed itself over behind me as I crouched, surrounded
by millions of beetles at their weird woodworking,
dressing the sacrificial pillar in ritual scars
as the light began to fade, green to grey to black. . . .

Soon after true dawn, we felt the idle sun begin
interrogation without mercy through the window's lens.

Cleaning the gutters, I uncovered an inchling elm
sprouting in a film of silt, the parent's misplaced
attempt to continue its line, one of a seed-billow
mostly squandered on the sidewalk. But after a week
in prime light and conditions, the blight emerges
even in offspring so slight, its proto-leaves flawed.
"If a tree dies, then plant another in its place,"
said Linnaeus, healthy logic for a dying elm or man
though in the end, no matter how prolific, nothing
can save us from ourselves, the inner and outer laws—
our seeds so frail, borne on silly wings and tails!

I have seen the vast redwoods, driven through one,
posed for pictures by another trying to capture
a sense of scale: failed, naturally, the photo
a mere section of its colossal trunk, useless
as truncated attempts to frame Salisbury's tower
intact, myself a microscopic tourist squinting
toward the spire invisible as deity itself.

And I have hooped (with three lusty others)
a Nantahala poplar, one of Kilmer's virgin stand—
the power of chastity obvious there, birdsong
a mere rumor in the canopy, sunshine and wind
so faint it felt like the bottom of the sea.
Ghostly chestnuts, wiped out by blight long ago,
lay as they fell, trunks flung from splintered
pediments of stump, like a Confederate battlefield
with the dead at attention in dress gray, ready
to cross white water to that other, bluer side.

Our elm, no less the wonder of its world, now sprawls
across the scrubby lot, a memento mori, its stump
still standing at martyred chestnut-height, periscope
from the underworld, the netherlands where roots rot
and the radical dead, restless beneath their plot
of petrified stumps, pray to rise into real trees.

Mr. Green's widow—so painfully scarred from a fire
she could hardly suffer clothes, though when she did
always appeared in long-sleeved dress and fine wig—
plucks his bean vines in the noon heat. She continues
her extravagant watering of his peas and tomatoes
stewing on the vine, these vegetables his memorial,
the last thing he set his hand to. "It is a good sign,"
the preacher had said, "when a dying man plants tomatoes."
As she bends to weed again, she smiles and seems to speak,
feeling her husband's shade comfort her down the row.

Coming home, we drove through Sunday countryside.
Several small churches had spread their homecoming
under funeral tents and a solitary elm, welcoming back
dispersed congregations, family trees pruned, scattered,
now regathered, even backsliders. Wide plank tables sat
swayback with food, favorite and secret recipes, ham,
burnished chicken, fresh-picked vegetables, desserts
staggering in their variety, more than any paper plate
or stomach could bear. After "Blest Be the Tie" sung
arm-in-arm, and a general grace, the people circulate
under the tree, laughing and crying and feasting
as if under the cool sheltering wings of the Almighty.
Having endured, through open windows, an eternity
of sermons and revivals, having outlived generations
of members remembered in stone rows on the hill,
having seen the church refined from logs to boards
to affluent brick, the tree more than any thing
built by human hands is the everlasting heart
of this homecoming, every spreading tree the core
of some return home, the remnant elm still rising
into a pillar of living fire for the chosen people,
its bark of life blazed with deep lovesick initials,
the focus of their story, their glory and their crown.

A NOTE ON THE AUTHOR

MICHAEL MCFEE'S poems and essays have appeared
in *The New Yorker, Poetry, Parnassus: Poetry in
Review,* and many other publications; his first book
of poetry was *Plain Air* (University Presses of
Florida, 1983). He has won fellowships in poetry
from the National Endowment for the Arts, the
Ingram Merrill Foundation, and the North Carolina
Arts Council, as well as the Discovery/ *The Nation*
award and a Pushcart Prize. A member of the
National Book Critics Circle, he has been a visiting
poet at Cornell, Lawrence, UNC-Greensboro,
UNC-Chapel Hill, and the Duke University Writers'
Conference.

A NOTE ON THE BOOK

Vanishing Acts was composed in Bembo
with Eric Gill's Perpetua used for
display. Composition by Graphic
Composition, Inc. It was printed
on acid-free paper by Thomson-
Shore, Inc. in an edition of
1,000 copies.